John Hopkins Morison

**Two sermons preached in the First Congregational church in**

**Milton on the 15th and 22d of June, 1862**

John Hopkins Morison

**Two sermons preached in the First Congregational church in Milton on the 15th and 22d of June, 1862**

ISBN/EAN: 9783337113575

Printed in Europe, USA, Canada, Australia, Japan

Cover: Foto ©Lupo / pixelio.de

More available books at **www.hansebooks.com**

# TWO SERMONS

PREACHED IN THE

## First Congregational Church

IN

# MILTON,

ON

THE 15th AND 22d OF JUNE, 1862,

AND

SUGGESTED BY

## THE CENTENNIAL CELEBRATION,

ON

## THE 11th OF JUNE, 1862.

By JOHN H. MORISON, D. D.

BOSTON:

JOSEPH G. TORREY, PRINTER, 32 CONGRESS STREET.

1862.

# PREFACE.

These are not historical discourses. The strictly historical part of our Centennial Celebration was ably treated by Hon. James Murray Robbins, who understands thoroughly every thing that relates to the town, and whose father and grand-father filled a most important place in its history. What I have attempted is to awaken an interest in those who have gone before us by exhibiting as I might, in two sermons, some of the characteristics of the place, illustrating what I had to say by very slight biographical sketches. I have thrown into the form of notes a few other facts, of little interest to strangers, but which may have a meaning and a value here. There are very subtle chains of association which bind togeth-er the generations of those who live in the same neighborhood, and make them from first to last, one living organization, so that something of the same spirit flows through and animates them all. We have as little of this personal identity as any com-munity that I have known. And yet there is a sense in which it does exist, and these discourses are given to the friends who have kindly asked for them in the hope that in some small way, they may help to connect us more closely with those who have gone before us, and lead us to look forward with new interest and increased efforts for their improvement to those who shall come after us to dwell amid these beautiful works of God when we are dead.

# SERMON.

One generation passeth away, and another generation
cometh.—Ecclesiastes 1 : 4.

I propose to dwell this morning on a few considerations suggested by the recent Celebration in this town. We, — those who are and those who have been residents in this place, — have met together during the last week with appropriate services to commemorate our history for the past two centuries. As I was listening to the instructive and excellent discourse that was delivered here, the first thing that struck me was the similarity of features that marked the history and character of our people from the earliest settlement of the place. One generation has passed away, another has come. Those born here have gone to distant places, and strangers have entered into the homes which they left. Very few homesteads are occupied now by the direct descendants of those who first settled here, and yet the marked characteristics of the people are to-day very much what they were half a century or a century and a half ago. The town is not and never has been one community. It is made up, and from the beginning it has been made up, from nearly all the classes of society that are to be found in the State. During the last sixteen years, at every election, I think, the vote in this town has pretty fairly represented the vote of the whole State, so that when the vote of Milton is declared, we know very well what is the vote of Massachusetts. Nearly all interests, professions and pursuits are represented here in just about the same proportion to each other as in the State. This gives us, and from the beginning has given us, a various, and in some respects a heterogeneous population. We have fewer things in common than is usual in a small town. We are less compactly united. We have less a feeling of interest and pride in what relates to the town. A single fact will illustrate what I mean : The second officer in command of the great army now at Richmond — a man of distinguished military ability, who two weeks ago to-day, in the battle at Fair Oaks, by what seemed almost an impossibility, did more perhaps than any other man to save the fortunes of the day, was a Milton boy, — the son of Milton parents, and educated in our Milton schools. But I doubt whether there is another town in the United States, where such a fact would be so little regarded, and where on a public occasion like that of the last week, so little notice would be taken of a son so distinguished, and at this moment holding so important a post.

Our lines have fallen to us in pleasant places. We are attached to the natural features of the town. We love its hills and streams, its woods and meadows, and carry them, wherever we go, in our thoughts and our affections. We are thankful that our children should

be born and trained up with these beautiful works of
God around them. As Gov. Hutchinson, after he had
removed to England, is said to have longed and pined
for his pleasant home on Milton Hill, and never could
find any other spot to take its place in his affections,
so, many a native of this town, forced to go abroad and
find employment elsewhere, has always turned with
loving, longing heart towards this beautiful home
of his childhood. And yet it would, perhaps be hard
to find, living side by side, under the same local
institutions and laws, in a country town, the same
number of persons bound together by so slight a community of feeling, or of social intercourse. And so
apparently it has been from the beginning. Peter
Thacher, in 1681, speaks of the " lamentable animosities and divisions" which prevailed even at that early
period. There is, and has been no want of kind feeling. Individuals have had their personal friends. —
Families have had their ties and their gatherings.
But the mere relations of neighborhood have been almost ignored. In the interest which a community
usually takes in its own sons, in the encouragement
with which it follows them in a career of honorable
exertion, in the sympathy which it feels for them in
their reverses, in the care with which it treasures up
the memory of their high qualities and praise-worthy
acts, this town has been unlike any other town that I
have known. And I cannot but hope that the celebration of the last week, by reviving the memory of
the past, by reminding us how much we have in common and how greatly our social privileges are increased by sharing them with others, may do some-

8

thing to create and perpetuate the feeling which should
bind each one of us, not only to the soil on which he
was born, but to the community in which he lives,—
leading us to recognize and hold in honor the virtues
of its children, and to encourage them with the thought
that here at least their good deeds and names will be
held in proud and grateful remembrance. Such a
community of feeling here, greeting the child when he
first enters our schools, watching over him with a kind
and almost parental interest, rejoicing in his successes,
following him wherever he goes, is among the most
grateful and effective encouragements that can be extended to the young. There is something of this feeling among us. There are those in whose opening virtues and graces we have taken an honest pride and
satisfaction. There are faithful ones among us here
whose promise of future usefulness is a joy to many
hearts. And there are young men of spotless lives —
modest and brave and true — now at their posts of
honor and of danger afar off, whom we can hardly
think of without a glow of emotion, and a secret prayer
for their safety and success.

Our thoughts are naturally carried back to the ele-
ments of our New England society. First, there was
the Church. The church which came over to Plymouth in the Mayflower was in itself a complete and
independent organization, and a type of all the rest.
According to his words who has said, " Wherever two
or three are gathered together in my name there am I
in the midst of them," those devout men and women
had come together in their Master's name, and bound
themselves together by a religious compact which has

served as a type of our whole civil polity. After the
pattern of the church was the town, with its local institutions and laws, a separate and almost independent
organization, so that, if it should be cut off, as the Plymouth colony was for a time, from all other communities and sovereignties, it might have in itself the right
to execute all the functions of civil government. These
townships, borrowing their life as they did, in our
early history, from the church, are the peculiar feature
of our New England civilization. More than three-
quarters of the money spent and of the most important
legislation of the country is decided upon in these pri-
mary meetings of the people, and they alone, self-sup-
porting and self-regulating as they are, make a repub-
lic like ours possible.

But the town organization is made possible only by
the more vital influences which are at work within itself. Of these, the Christian church has held the
most important place. It has been made in no small
measure the medium of religious instruction and religious life to each individual soul. Its divine spirit enters the school, and makes knowledge a power, not for
evil, but for good. It enters the home, purifies its affections, softens its asperities, consecrates the marriage
ties, welcomes the little child into its bosom, opens its
blessed promises to the dying, and lifts up the hearts of
the sorrowing by its words of immortal faith at the
very portals of the tomb.

Say what we may of the stern creed of our ancestors, and its hardening influence on harsh and ungainly
natures, it was not all harshness. In the sentiment of
reverance which it fostered, in the habit which it en-

2

couraged of looking with profound and earnest thought into the solemn and awful mysteries of our religion, in the unshrinking courage with which it accepted whatever it believed to be a divine truth, however severe its exactions, it cultivated some of the sublimest qualities which belong to the human character. Those ancient men who first trod these roads and looked upon these hills, or gazed off upon the distant waters, carried with them a faith which made the earth the footstool of God's throne, and themselves the chosen servants of God to establish here in the wilderness a divinely ordered commonwealth, rich in all the promises and fruits of holy living.

And the milder virtues were not forgotten or despised. The pastors of this church, from the beginning, were men of gentle, benignant characters. Peter Thacher, who lived near the brook, perhaps a third of a mile back from the spot where we now are, was a man whose daily walk with God was shown more in the graces and charities of a Christian life than in the severe teachings of a harsh and ungracious theology. He was the son of a Christian minister and the father almost of a race of ministers, some of them distinguished for intelligence and wit, but upon the whole characterized by a winning gentleness of speech and of life. I love to think of this good man, forty-seven years the minister of Christ in this town, in simplicity and godly sincerity having his conversation among his people, preaching and praying and living among them and for them, burying all the first generation of settlers and almost all of their children—till at length, having grown old in their service, he appeared for the last time

in the church. "He preached," says Cotton Mather
in his funeral sermon, "both parts of the day, [he also
baptized two children,] felt more hearty than ordinary,
and performed the domestic services, with the repetition
of the sermons, in the evening. Upon which finding
himself weary, he said, 'we read in a certain place, the
prayers of David are ended, what if it should now be
said, the prayers of Peter are ended.' It fell out accordingly. On the day following a fever seized him, and
the next Sabbath ended with him in his everlasting rest."

"In the time of his illness he expressed a most lovely acquiescence in the will of his heavenly Father, and
a soul rejoicing in the hope of the glory of God."

I know not where to find a more beautiful picture
of Patriarchal dying than is given of him in his last
hour. "Recovering," says Cotton Mather, "out of a
short cloud, upon the clear use of his reason, he called
for his domestics and for a staff to lean upon. So sitting up, he blessed each of them, and made a most
pathetic and audible prayer with them and for them.
And then lying down, his last words were the words
of a conqueror, and more than a conqueror, 'I am going to Christ in glory.' Thus his purified spirit flew
away to the chambers of a Redeemer waiting to be
gracious. He died in the calm with which he lived, and
expired with no groans but those of one longing to be
with Him, with whom to be is by far the best of all."

His successor, John Taylor, was settled here at the
age of twenty-five, and died when only forty-six years
old. He was evidently a man of mild deportment,
and of engaging personal qualities  I have read his
letters written through a series of years, to his father in-

law, in Portsmouth, N. H. They give evidence of an affectionate, devout and thoughtful man. They are perhaps a little more formal than would be in keeping now with the habits of the age, but give no indication of the moroseness or severity which we are too apt to attribute to the clergymen of that generation. He was evidently a Christian gentleman and scholar. His heart was in his work. He loved his people, and rejoiced to labor for their good. The only work of his which is now visible among us — the house which he built and which is still occupied by his kindred—bears witness to his taste. He was cut down in the prime of his manhood, and in the midst of his labors, and was mourned over and lamented by his people as one who had endeared himself to them by his fidelity, and his thoughtful, affectionate care for them.

He was succeeded by Nathaniel Robbins, who was settled at the age of twenty-four in 1750, and who continued the minister of the town for a period of forty-five years, closing his ministerial labors with his life in 1795. From all that I can learn of him, he was a man of a most genial nature, more ready to perform a kind act for a neighbor than to rebuke him for wrong doing, working upon his farm as well as in his study, more intent on the practical duties of our religion than its mysterious doctrines, a lover of peace and concord, and doing what he could to remove all uncharitableness and to promote harmony and good will among his people. He did not dislike a harmless joke, and was always, I believe, a man of a cheerful, happy disposition, a pleasant companion, and a beloved pastor.

These three ministries reach thro' a period of a

hundred and fourteen years, and come down almost to
to the close of the last century. They witnessed great
and momentous changes in the history of our country.
Thacher was born in 1651, when we were in the feeble and exposed days of our infancy. Robbins was
here during the stormy period of our revolutionary
history, when his people knew what it was to make
sacrifices for their country. It is said that one woman
in his parish — a widow — used to sit knitting before
her door, by the brook, which still bears her name,
when the weather would permit, and asked of any
stranger who passed by, " What 's the news from the
war? I have four sons gone to the war — what 's
the news from the war ?" One of her sons was Col.
another the Lieut. Col. of the 1st Mass. Regiment,
while the other two served perhaps as faithfully in
more humble capacities. So our fathers lived in this
beautiful town, working out the great problem of life
each in his own way, serving God according to their
light in their day and generation. And it becomes us
who have entered into their labors to hold them in
grateful and affectionate remembrance.

There are some points of a more private and domestic character which I wish to dwell upon. But
that must be deferred till the next Sunday. A word
more at this time. I have spoken of the first three
ministers of this town. Hardly more than two or three
persons are now among us who remember the last of
these men. More than four generations have passed
away since the saintly life of Thacher was closed by
his triumphant death. A large elm has grown from
the cellar of the house in which he died. All the men

and children whom his eyes looked upon have gone. Their children's children are among the generations that have passed away, and no tradition respecting him, except in books, is preserved here in what was the field of his labors for almost half a century. But that death bed scene which I have presented in the dying words of his friend — for his funeral sermon was the last sermon that Cotton Mather ever preached — that victorious faith of his and of those who succeeded him— the inspiration and the fruits of many labors and prayers—lifting them above the world and leading them triumphantly on from things seen and temporal to things unseen and eternal, they speak to us, not of the generations that pass away, but of joys and souls which endure forever. Like those good men we must die. Our very names may be forgotten when the next centennial day shall be commemorated by those who come after us. All that our eyes now look upon will be nothing to us. Shall we not then by holy and faithful living, seek, like them, to secure for ourselves everlasting habitations in the kingdom of Christ.?

# SERMON.

MY SON, HEAR THE INSTRUCTION OF THY FATHER, AND FOR-
SAKE NOT THE LAW OF THY MOTHER: FOR THEY SHALL BE
AN ORNAMENT OF GRACE UNTO THY HEAD, AND CHAINS ABOUT
THY NECK. Proverbs 1: 8, 9.

LAST Sunday I spoke of the social condition of this
town in some of the more extended relations, and especially of the church and its doctrines. illustrating the
latter part of the subject by slight sketches of the three
ministers who came within the first century of our history.

I wish this morning to speak of some of our private
and domestic relations. Wherever there are happy
and virtuous homes, there, more than any where else,
the great purposes of human society and of human life
are accomplished. In these homes woman must ne-
cessarily be the presiding and tutelary genius. Not
only the softening graces and accomplishments which
adorn the character and lend their charm to society
come from her, but the hardier virtues, which defend
the state and stay off the streams of public corruption
that are perpetually making inroads on private morals,
find their inspiration and support in the training which
the young man has first received in the home of his
childhood.

The ablest philosophical writer of the present century on this class of subjects, Alexis de Tocqueville, [Democracy in America. Part Second, New York, 1840,] after asserting [Chap. viii,] that "no free communities ever existed without morals," that "morals are the work of woman," and that all travellers who have visited North America, however they differ in other things, agree that morals are far more strict here than elsewhere, the Americans being in this respect very much superior to the English, concludes his remarks on this subject [Chap. xii, p. 227,] with this emphatic declaration : "I have nowhere seen women occupying a loftier position ; and if I were asked, now that I am drawing to the close of this work in which I have spoken of so many important things done by the Americans, to what the singular prosperity and growing strength of that people ought mainly to be attributed, I should reply — to the superiority of their women."

This remark of the ablest philosophical thinker and observer who has ever written on American society and institutions is unquestionably correct, and its truth may be verified in the history even of a little community like this.

But if we attempt to go back more than a century, it is impossible to get at the details which are necessary in order to an intelligent and satisfactory treatment of the subject. Examples of domestic virtue live and reign within their own limited sphere. In their obscure retreats, as in so many private laboratories, they mould the characters of the young, and thus prepare the forces which are to act on public institutions and laws. A young lad at school in Andover, eighty years ago, saw a poor wretch, publicly whipped before the house in which he boarded. Other boys very likely regarded the suffering criminal with laughter and mockery. The lady of the house, Mrs. Phillips, whose husband was one of the founders of Phillips Academy, told this boy that if he lived to be a man and had any influence as a legislator, she hoped he would have that shameful and degrading punishment abolished. Very early in life the boy became a statesman, and one of his early acts was to have that blot erased from the statute book of his native State.

The author of this act happened to be mentioned; but in ninety-nine cases out of a hundred, she who has furnished the motive, and is really the originator of the beneficent step that is taken in the onward progress of the race, goes to her grave unrecognized as such by others, and without any suspicion in her own mind of the good that she has done. And the fact that it is woman's province thus to work in privacy, like a fair taper, as has been said, shining to all the room, but casting a modest shadow around herself,—the fact that she should thus be the inspiration of so much that is good to others while she claims so little for herself, is one of the causes which give her such a hold on the affections and the admiration of men.

But those, whose lives are thus spent, leave little for the historian to record. They are satisfied to live unknown beyond their own quiet sphere. What is best in them transfuses itself into those around them and lives on in their lives. The homes which they have filled and cheered with their presence feel that their light has gone out when they die. Their children arise up and call them blessed. Grand children retain in their hearts some pleasant memorials of what they were, and perhaps always feel as if a mild and hallowed illumination had passed out of their sky when they departed. But after that no record of what they were remains. The places which knew them and which were dearer to them than to any one else, know them no more forever, and transmit to us no glimpse of the lives they lived, as distinguished from the lives of others.

Hence it is impossible to illustrate what I wish to say by examples which do not come down pretty nearly to the memory of persons now living. Peter Thacher died a hundred and thirty-five years ago ; and we have quite a distinct view of his character and life. But of the wife of his youth,—"My dear wife Theodora," as he calls her in the church records, — daughter of Rev. John Oxenbridge, of Boston, and the mother of nine children — we have scarcely any account beyond this inscription on her tomb stone :

M<sup>RS</sup> THEODORA THACHER Y̆ DAUGHTER
OF Y̆ REV<sup>D</sup> M<sup>R</sup> JOHN OXENBRIDGE PASTOR
OF Y̆ FIRST CHURCH IN BOSTON & WIFE
OF M<sup>R</sup> PETER THACHER   AGED 38 YEARS
3 MONTHES 23 DAYES WAS TRANSLATED
FROM EARTH TO HEAVEN NOV<sup>R</sup> Y̆ 18 1697.

We visit the houses that were built during the first century after the settlement of the town. We see enough there to confute the idea which some entertain that those who built them were persons without taste or

culture. Almost without exception they occupy sites
as pleasant as the town affords, and in their position
and architectural finish show a degree of skill and a delicacy of taste which have hardly been exceeded in our
day. Those who dwelt in them had many privations
which we know nothing of. The hardships of their
lot bore, as they usually do in new settlements, with
unequal severity on the women. But they had their
delicacies and refinements. On great occasions their
garments, which often lasted more than a lifetime, and
were handed down as heir-looms from one generation
to another, were of more costly materials, and made
up with a more elaborate finish, than their successors
in the same walks of life now would indulge in. In
their social intercourse they were more dignified and
stately than our customs would authorize. The different ranks of society and the tokens of respect due from
one to another were more precisely marked out than
in our day. If the higher classes exacted more from
those below them, they were ready to do more for
them in return, and to defend them from the exactions
or oppressions of the powerful.

There is no picture of the past so attractive to me as
that of a Christian home. In carrying our thoughts
back to the early settlers at times when every nerve
was strained to meet the physical wants of the day,
we see that there was always found a season, not only
in the church for public worship, but at home for
prayer and religious instruction, and the cultivation of
those inward graces which draw together the members
of a household by something stronger than the ties of
interest or habit, and throw over the opening intelli-

gence of the child visions more sacred and inspiring
than the earth can give. In those visions of heavenly
glory, those thoughts of near access and solemn ac-
countability to God, the child's whole nature was
bathed and made alive. They touched the inmost
springs and motives of conduct, and moulded his views
and habits of life. While the characters thus fash-
ioned were to some extent marked by the severity
which grew out of the theology of the age and the
hardships to which the men were exposed, they were
also filled with the tender sympathies and affections
which are always cherished by a heartfelt intercourse
with God, and which cannot be separated from the religious nurture of a Christian home.

In each of these homes, the presiding genius and
divinity of the place was the Christian mother. She
was the centre of kindly influences and attractions.
Out of door cares and toils tasked to the utmost the
time and strength of the father. But she, not less
heavily burdened with bodily labor,— even in her sor-
rows perhaps finding no leisure for grief, but working, and weeping while she worked,— was always
there, the dignity of her outward demeanor subdued
by the solicitudes and yearnings which drew her towards her children. Amid the hardness which might
have been caused by the severity of their creed, or the
stern necessities which pressed upon them and hem-
med them in, here was a never failing fountain, opening within their homes, and supplying them with the
soft, sweet waters of domestic peace. The birth of a
child was a new evangel, calling into exercise all the
tenderness and strength of a mother's heart. Her self-

denying virtues, her conjugal affections, her intelligence, her faith, in itself the evidence of things not seen, and the deeper religion of the heart, were all employed in her domestic relations. "When my mother comes from her chamber where she has been praying," said a young man of rare intellectual and moral gifts, " her face is like the face of an angel." So has many a mother been glorified in the eyes of her children.

And such were the mothers whom we love to look back upon as the pride and glory of the days that are gone. They, under God, formed the great men, who by their far seeing wisdom, their strong wills, and sublime faith, were always equal to the emergencies of their time, who elevated the tone of public morals, enlarged the intelligence and strengthened the virtues of the age in which they lived, and thus laid here, on this North American continent, the foundations of a mighty empire, so deep and firm that neither the passions of wicked men nor the gates of hell shall prevail against it.

It is the merciful infusion of domestic love and kindness that saves men from becoming a race of infidels and savages. Man gladly accepts the aid of a nature more delicate than his own, more open to religious impressions. and to the finer influences that are around us. While he seems to be the controlling mind, he willingly subjects himself to her finer instincts. In recognizing the original differences of organization between the sexes, he joyfully acknowledges her superiority in some things, as he practically asserts his own superiority in others. By adjusting itself to constitutional diversities, and seeking harmony in variety, gaining mutual support by mutual submission and respect, society here in New England has done much, though much remains to be done, to make the position of woman honorable, and her influence what it should be. Relations thus mutually helpful, affections kept alive by acts of kindness every day reciprocated, cannot be otherwise than blessed. The longer they continue, the more alive they are. And when, after a long union, the connection seems to be dissolved by death, then all the more touching is the pathos of the separation, and the stronger the assurance which the heart finds of a re-union. An aged woman whom I knew, gazing tearfully on the face of her husband who had just ceased to breathe at the age of eighty-five or eighty-seven years, exclaimed, " O Billy, Billy, shall I never hear your voice again ? We have lived together more than fifty years, and I never heard from you an unkind word." I was with a man eighty-four years old who supposed himself to be, as he was, almost on the borders of eternity. " I would gladly die," he said, " if I could only be sure of meeting my wife " — who had died some years before — " and knowing her again." These are the feelings fostered by long lives of mutual fidelity and kindness in the dearest domestic relations. They give the assurance of peace and happiness on earth, and reach on in hope and love to that world where ties apparently broken here shall be united again.

It would be easy to carry out this theme, with variations, by examples drawn from those who have been trained and nurtured here. But I must allow myself a wider range. The happy influence of our homes, especially in the character of the women who have presided over them, or whom they have produced, are best illustrated by the examples which we have found in the seclusion of domestic life.

Near the Railway village, under the shadow of an ancient elm, is a pleasant one story house with a gambrel roof, where sixty years ago were seven sisters, who were all in due time educated in the usual branches of learning, all taught, as every young woman should be, to support themselves by the work of their own hands. The only one now living among us is the oldest person belonging to this church, and, I think, the oldest person in Milton. All of them have been wives and mothers, and all but two have gone from their earthly labors, after having fulfilled with singular fidelity the duties of a Christian wife and mother. One of them, the wife of an accomplished teacher, exercised a happy and extended influence over the young, and of another the following words were written by Dr. Channing in a private letter soon after her death :

"It was not necessary to see her often to know and love her. The simplicity, sweetness, delicacy, and purity of her spirit shone out in her countenance too brightly to be overlooked, even by a stranger. I remember when I was in —— three or four years ago I rode with —— to visit her at her residence. It was after her husband's failure, and to this misfortune had been added the sickness of her family, — I think intermittent fever, taken in an unhealthy spot, to which they had retreated after his losses. Here was an accumulation of calamity, and her frame bore the mark of exhausting labor. But a more lovely manifestation of a resigned spirit I never witnessed. The tear trembled in her eye, as she told me of their trials; but a sweet smile said in the most unequivocal language, — 'His will be done.' I had that morning visited some choice paintings brought by a very opulent friend from Europe, which had given me much pleasure; but on returning to the carriage after my interview with your sister, I said,— I have seen and admired a great deal of beauty this morning, but in all those works of genius I have seen nothing so beautiful as the friend we have just left. That expression of ———'s countenance remains with me, and it cheers and consoles me at this moment. There was something heavenly in that spirit, and that cannot die."

I wish to speak of another Milton woman whose example is worthy of all commendation. A little way from the spot where we are assembled, in a lane now closed, just this side of the Amory place, in a house of which no remnants remain, was born, one of five sisters, Miss Ann Bent, who died a few years ago at the age of eighty-nine. She began to support her father's family by teaching a school of little children on Milton Hill. Afterward she opened a shop in Boston where she supported herself many years, teaching other young women to do the same, and, in addition to the many kind and charitable acts in which she greatly delighted, she laid up an abundant competency for her old age. She numbered among her personal friends many of the most cultivated and excellent persons in Boston. Her house was the unostentatious and attractive centre of a pleasant society of refined, religious minded people. She always found occupation for her benevolent sympathies. She lived a happy, useful, honored life amid the affections of others, and died lamented and beloved. Few persons among us have done more to enlarge the field of reputable industry for woman, to show that she can be respected and happy without being married, that by her own exertions she can create and support a home where. without the assistance of one bound by law to honor and provide for her, she may, down to the latest period of a long life, protect herself from injuries or neglect by her own virtues and graces, and, without the hereditary homage of children and children's children, find herself looked up to with increasing respect, and cared for by increasing affections which turn fondly towards her, and gladly pay back, in acts of loving gratitude, the debt they owe.

The fourth minister of this parish was Joseph McKean. He was born in Boston and ordained here at the early age of twenty-one. He was a man of unusual intellectual gifts, ardent, faithful and unwearied. He sought the highest good of the town and church. But his activities were too large for his place and flowed over into other departments. He entered with all the zeal of his energetic nature into the political contests of the day, and sometimes used his keen powers of ridicule and sarcasm in speaking of parishioners who opposed him on political grounds. We owe to his laborious care the fact that we have left any record of the early doings of our church. After an efficient and successful, though somewhat troubled, ministry of seven years, he resigned his charge on account of impaired health. He took a voyage to the South. He

4

preached a year or two very acceptably in Boston,
Milton being still for the most part his home. He
succeeded John Quincy Adams as Professor of Rhet-
oric and Oratory at Harvard College in 1809, and dis-
charged the duties of his post there with signal ability
and success till his death in 1818, at the age of forty-
two. He was a man of marked influence and character, to be remembered by those who knew him. I
had some little acquaintance with his widow who
survived him many years. She was a woman of singular sweetness of nature, refined and gentle. thoroughly feminine in all her qualities, devout, confiding, affectionate, and yet, if I mistake not, very firm in her
convictions, and with a quiet resolution which was
not easily turned aside from what she might think it
her duty to undertake. She lived amid the devoted
affections of her children and friends.

I might speak of other women, in widely different
spheres of life, who were her contemporaries and friends
here, and who illustrated in different ways some of the
best characteristics of our New England culture.
There have been those among us whose freedom show-
ed itself in painful excentricities. But there were a
few living when I came here, whom I was glad to recognize as the honored survivers and representatives
of a former generation. It was a privilege to be with
them, and to look on them as mediators and ambassa-
dors to us from a former century. As beloved and
venerated monuments of the past, they carried our
thoughts back to a time of greater simplicity in the
habits of living, of a more courteous, and, I must add,
a more attractive dignity of manners, as well as to a

time of severe duties and harder struggles than are common now. Through them we were permitted to recall the image of former days, to catch something of the delicate hue and perfume of those earlier times, to converse of persons whose characters were formed before our country had yet an independent place or name among the nations, to dwell with them amid the virtues which made those days illustrious, and to admire in them the calm dignity which comes from a true elevation of mind and heart, and a courtesy which in its own Christian self respect never forgot what was due to the feelings and the self respect of others. But I must not single them out one by one, and dwell upon their memory as I should be glad to do for our sake more than for theirs.

Yes, these homes have been inhabited, these fields have been frequented, these roads have been travelled by those whom it is a joy and a privilege to remember,— women who made the atmosphere in which they lived fragrant with their affections, their prayers, and their graceful and gracious deeds. Some have just begun to reveal to us the beautiful promise of what they might be and have passed away, leaving with us only the pleasant vision of a loveliness on which the bloom and freshness of a perpetual youth will linger in our thoughts till we meet them above in all the radiance of their celestial being. Others have gone from us in the mellowness of a ripened old age. Others again, and among them some of the finest specimens of womanhood that we have known, went away in the fulness of all their powers.

One of these I will mention, because not only she,

but every member of her household is gone. She was a child of this town, born to affluence, the child of her father's old age and the favored object of his indulgence, — early a member of this church — a faithful pains-taking teacher in our Sunday school, and gratefully remembered as such by pupils whose grateful remembrance is indeed a benediction — a wife and a mother with everything apparently that this world has to give at her command — giving and receiving the most constant and devoted acts of love and kindness— then watching the failing health of the one dearest to her, with anxious solicitude — "bereft of light"— a widow, following first a child and then a mother to the grave. Yet she lived on, walked abroad amid objects dear to her, but seeing them only in her thoughts. She loved, as few persons have, every thing belonging to this town — its hills, its streams and meadows, its trees and its people — taking a kindly interest in every thing that occurred, her sympathies confined to no one class, glad to do what she might for all. When she died, the light of hope and love shone more dimly in many a home and heart which she had cheered by the gentle illumination of her sympathy and kindness. And now not one of all her household lives on earth. At the close of this second century, as we bind our wreaths of loving remembrance and lay them softly on the tombs of those who have been our friends and benefactors, who have meekly fulfilled the duties of life and passed on where they rest from their labors and their works do follow them, we may bind up this frail memorial of personal respect and gratitude, and lay it on a grave which no descendant of hers shall ever visit.

Yes, tender and hallowed memories gather round us as we look back through these completed centuries. To you it is one thing; to me who came recently among you it is another. Yet to all of us it is the same. Dear forms, no longer among the living, come thronging back to us. Dear lives, which have vanished wholly from sight, but whose sweetness lingers still in our hearts, revive again, and give us anew their holy benison. So may this season of commemoration touch all our hearts, draw us on to more holy and faithful living, till we too shall join that silent company of God's elect, and be numbered with them among the saints in glory.

## THE FIRST CONGREGATIONAL CHURCH IN MILTON.

The Church in Milton was gathered April 24, 1678. The Covenant then entered into was signed by the following names.

| | |
|---|---|
| ANTHONY NEWTON, | EBENEZER CLAP, |
| ROBERT TUCKER, | EDWARD BLACKE, |
| WILLIAM BLACKE, | GEORGE LION, |
| THOMAS SWIFT, | JAMES TUCKER, |
| GEORGE SUMNER, | EPHRAIM TUCKER, |
| THOMAS HOLMAN, | MANASSAH TUCKER, |

On Sunday, the eighth of May, 1681, Mr. Peter Thacher, who had been invited to become the pastor of the church and town, after the exercises of the Sabbath, read to the church and congregation his reply accepting their call, on these conditions :

" 1. So long as you continue one amongst yourselves and for me all due means being used or tendred for hearing in case of differance."

" 2. So long as I may enjoy the liberty of my judgment according to scripture rule."

" 3. So long as you subject yourselves and yours to the ordinances and officers of this church."

" 4. So long as I may follow my studdys without distraction ; and provide for myself and family according to the rules of God's word," &c., &c.

Among the first entries of members admitted to the church, in Mr. Thacher's handwriting, are the following :

"4 April, 1681. Peter Thacher by a letter of dismission from the third church in Boston, was admitted."

" June 1, 1681. Peter Thacher, [though unworthy,] was ordained Pastor of the church of Milton."

"Oct. 2, 1681. My dear wife Theodora Thacher was admitted into full communion makeing a relation."

Mr. Thacher had removed his family to Milton before making up his mind to settle here. In his letter, or rather address of acceptance, he says ; " I was persuaded so far to comply with all as to remove myself and my family to this place, that so I might the more clearly discern and faithfully follow divine guidance and direction in my future settlement amongst you or remove from you, according as God should unite the harts of the church and congregation unto me and mine and ours unto you, or otherwise dispose." He had hesitated long before accepting the invitation, not only from a sense of his " own deep unworthiness" and " great unfitness " for the work of the ministry, " but especially in this place," he adds, " in respect of those lamentable animosityes and divisions which have been in this place, which hath occasioned your unsettlement until now, which the Lord for his own name sake pardon, and prevent for the future " His prayer seems to have been answered ; for the affairs of the society seem to have been favored with an extraordinary degree of harmony for more than a hundred years from that time.

I copy a few items from the Church Records which may seem a little strange to us in these days.

" Nov. 24, 1695. Samuel, the son of George Summer was baptized. This George was Left'nt G. S. eldest son, and this day hee did explicitely renew his covenant with God and y$^e$ Chh.

" Aug. 10, 1701. Margaret, my Indian maid joyned hers. to the Lord in a perpetuall covenant was taken under the watch and discipline of y$^e$ Chh. by a Chh. vote and so was baptized."

Feb. 1, 1718-9. Hagar my negro woman made her confession of her sin— and entered into covenant with God and came under y$^e$ watch and discipline of this Chh. and so was baptized and her children Sambo and Jimme were baptized at the same time."

" June 1727. Content Marah was baptized Hannah she requesting that her name might be changed "

" July 1, 1683. Henry Craine Seni'r rec'd, w$^c$ was y$^e$ first time I went abroad after my great sicknesse."

The last entry made by Mr. Thacher in the church records is as follows :

" Dec. 10, 1727. George y$^e$ son of Mr. Georg Badcock was baptized."

" Item. William the son of Mr. William Peirce was baptized, Dec. 10, 1727."

The next entry is the following, apparently in the handwriting of his successor :

" The Rev'd Mr. Peter Thacher (after above 46 years eminent service in the Ministerial office in the town of Milton,) died on y$^e$ 17th of Dec'r 1727. Blessed are the dead y$^t$ die in the Lord."

Rev. John Taylor was ordained Nov. 13, 1728. The following entry in his handwriting is found immediately under the original Covenant of the church.

" Dea. Manasseh Tucker (who was the last Survivour of the first set of Ch. Members) died April 9th, 1743.

"And as all that generation were gathered to their fathers, the church passed a vote (April 17) that they would renew Covenant with God and one another ; which they did accordingly, April 24th, when the members of the Ch. Male and Female, manifested their consents to their Fathers Covenant by standing up while I read it over with a small variation as the change of circumstances required. J. T."

The last entry made by Mr. Taylor in the church records, is among the baptisms, " Dec. 31, [1750,] Hephsibah, Daught. of Enoch Horton," and immediately below it is the following :

"The Rev'd Mr. John Taylor, after above 21 Years eminent Service in the Ministerial Office in y$^e$ town of Milton, Died on y$^e$ 26th Day of January, 1749-50. Blessed and forever happy are they wch die in y$^e$ Lord as well as those wch die for y$^e$ Lord."

Rev. Nathaniel Robbins was ordained Feb. 13, 1751.

He died May 19, 1795. The sermon at his funeral was preached by Rev. Jason Haven of Dedham. The Sunday following, a sermon which was afterwards printed, was preached by Rev. Thomas Thacher.

At a meeting, after divine services, June 19, 1796, the Church voted unanimously to invite Mr. John Pierce to become their Pastor. But the town did not concur with the Church. Mr. Pierce was afterwards the venerable and beloved Dr. Pierce of Brookline, where he sustained the relation of Pastor more than fifty years.

By one of the coincidences which Dr. Pierce loved to recognize, it so happened that he preached his last sermons here in the same church which had witnessed with warm approval his earliest labors in the sacred profession A glory passed away from our ministerial gatherings and from the Harvard College Commencements when his portly form, his benignant countenance, his white locks, his sonorous voice, and the pleasant contagion of his perpetual cheerfulness, had ceased from among us.

Rev. Joseph McKean was ordained Nov. 1, 1797. "Separated, at his proposal, on account of feeble health, and want of support, Oct. 3, 1804."

Rev. Samuel Gile was ordained Feb. 18, 1807. The latest entry in the church records which I find in his hand writing is Aug. 16, 1834, to record the death of Mrs. Abigail Swift, aged 76.

On account of difficulties about exchanges, which grew out of differences of opinion on doctrinal points, Mr. Gile's connection with the society was dissolved Jan. 6, 1834, through an Ex-parte Council called by the society, and composed of the following clergymen, Rev. Peter Whitney of Quincy, Rev. John White of West Dedham, Rev. Alvan Lamson, Dedham, Rev. James Walker, Charlestown, Rev. Lemuel Capen, South Boston, Rev. Samuel Barret, Boston.

Those of the parish who agreed with Mr. Gile in sentiment or who were drawn to him by a strong personal attachment formed a new society under the name of "The First Evangelical Society." He continued with them in the Ministerial office till the day of his death, Sunday, Oct. 16, 1836. He had preached in the morning, and when the congregation came together in the afternoon they heard of his sudden death during the intermission. Mr. Gile was a man of respectable abilities with a remarkable gift in prayer. He was beloved by his people, and at the time of the division in the parish, there was as little ill feeling as there ever is in such a separation, and he lived and died respected even by those who had felt it to be their duty to vote for his dismission. His widow lived till after these sermons were delivered, an object of tender regard to all who knew her, and looking with almost equal kindness upon all the families which had once been under her husband's ministry. She felt towards them all as a mother towards her children, and when she died, June 26, 1862, the remembrance of the life which she had led among them for more than fifty years, could awaken in those who had known her no other feeling than one of grateful and affectionate respect.

For nearly thirty years the two societies have held their meetings side by side, the church bells mingling together the sounds which call their respective worshipers to the house of prayer. They have labored, each in its own way and according to its own convictions, to do in this community the work which devolves on Christian societies. And if there have been any difficulties between them, or between their ministers, I have had no knowledge of it. If they have not worked together, they have worked in peace,—on one side, I am sure, and, I believe also, on the other, with sentiments of cordial good will. "Pray for the peace of Jerusalem : they shall prosper that love thee. Peace be within thy walls, and prosperity within thy palaces. For my brethren and companions sakes, I will now say, peace be within thee."

Rev. Benjamin Huntoon, having been unanimously called, was installed Pastor of the First Congregational Church and Society, Oct 15, 1834.

Introductory Prayer and reading Scriptures by Rev. George Putnam, of Roxbury. Prayer of Installation by Rev Peter Whitney of Quincy. Sermon by Rev. Thaddeus Mason Harris, D. D. of Dorchester. Charge by Rev. John Pierpoint of Boston. Right Hand of Fellowship by Rev. Francis Cunningham of Dorchester. Address to the People by Rev. Henry Ware, jr. D. D. of Cambridge. Concluding Prayer by Rev. John White of West Dedham.

Dec. 9th, 1835, "The old church having been turned round and thoroughly repaired, was reopened and dedicated to the service and worship of Almighty God. Rev. William P. Lunt of Quincy, and Rev. Orestes Brownson of Canton assisted Mr. Huntoon in the services.

Mr. Huntoon's connection with the society was dissolved at his own request, June 20, 1837, on account of his health, and that he might take charge of the Unitarian Society in Cincinnati. Mr. Huntoon went from Milton to Cincinnati ; Rev. Ephraim Peabody from Cincinnati to New Bedford, and Rev. Joseph Angier from New Bedford to Milton.

Rev. Joseph Angier was invited to become pastor of the society by a unanimous vote, Aug. 7, 1837, and was installed Sept. 13, 1837, Rev. Caleb Stetson of Medford preaching the sermon. At his own request, and against the wishes of the people, Mr. Angier's connection with the society was dissolved June 22, 1845.

The present pastor, John H. Morison, was installed Jan. 28, 1846.

From the first settlement of the town, notwithstanding the good Peter Thacher's fears about "the lamentable animosities and divisions, which has been in this place," the most remarkable feature in the history of the parish has been the harmony between the ministers and their people. From the time when the Call was given to Mr. Thacher in 1680 down to the present day, so far as the parish records show, there has been, with the single exception already mentioned, no difficulty between the minister and the parish. Mr. McKean and Mr. Gile were both settled by a unanimous vote of the Church. Every minister settled here since the division of the town has received a unanimous invitation from the parish, and when the connection has been dissolved it has been at the request of the Pastor and against the wishes of the Society.

It would be unjust to close this notice of the parish without speaking of the Sunday School to which it has owed no small part of its prosperity. For twenty years it was under the judicious care of Mr. Samuel Adams, who spared no labor or expense in its behalf, and who during those twenty years was only twice absent from his post at the opening of the services. He knew all the children of the parish. He visited the homes of the poor, supplied their wants, and from places too often neglected or forgotten, drew in children who would otherwise have been left to go astray. Those who were then connected with the school are not likely ever to forget their obligations to him.

The first Meeting House in Milton, I believe, stood near the place where Miss Polly Crane lived nearly ninety years of her long life, and where Mr. Wm. P. Blanchard now resides. The present Church was built in 1787. It was turned round in 1834, when the galleries were removed and a part of the building partitioned off as a Sunday School room. In 1851, the partition was removed so as to make room for twenty additional pews, and a new room was added for the Sunday School. At about the same time an organ was procured.

There are few finer situations for a country church, and the original advantages of the place have been greatly improved by the noble trees that stand upon it. About seventy years ago, at a town meeting, a number of young men agreed to spend the next day in setting out trees. They kept their engagement, and the fine elms which stand around the church with their hospitable shade and coolness through the summer months, and as holy sentinels amid the storms of winter, remain still the fruit of that one day's work, an emblem and memorial of the enduring results which may sometimes come from our transient exertions. This fact was told me by the late Gen. Moses Whitney, the last survivor of the company who transplanted the trees. Their names should be kept in lasting and pleasant remembrance.

## ANCIENT HOUSES AND ESTATES.

I can make out but five families who live now on land taken by their ancestors at the first settlement of the place. The widow of John Crehore holds a part of the original Crehore estate. The heirs of Simon and Rhoda [Kingsbury Sumner] Ferry live on land owned by their ancestors, the Sumners, from the beginning. Mr. Rufus P. Sumner cultivates, as his homestead, land which has been in his family from the earliest period of our history. The grandfather of the Hon. Charles Sumner was born and lived on some part of this Brush Hill Sumner estate. The Wadsworths, Jason, Thomas Thacher and Josiah, live on land which has never been out of the hands of their ancestors since it was first cultivated. The heirs of the late Col. Josiah H. Vose still occupy the place which has been owned by their family since 1654. And heirs of the late Mrs. Mary Boies Clark not only live on land owned by their ancestor, Robert Tucker, the first of the name in Milton, but it is probable that they live in the very house that he built a short time before his death. In his will made in 1682, he speaks of his "new house," and if that, as Mr. Robbins thinks, is the house now standing next beyond the Robbins house on Brush Hill, it must have been built as early as 1680, and is undoubtedly the oldest house in Milton. Next to it in age, and of a date not much more recent, is the Billings house. Both these houses are of a primitive order of architecture, and evidently belong to a period when building materials were plenty and labor was scarce. The Billings house continued in that family for many generations. Mr. William Crehore, whose mother was a Billings, and to whom I am indebted for many facts relating to our history, was born in this house more than 80 years ago, and at a much more recent period it was the birth-place of the distinguished architect, Mr. Charles Howland Hammatt Billings, son of Ebenezer Billings. The house was widely known as a public house before the beginning of the present century, and was a favorite place of resort, especially at the cherry and strawberry season, for parties from Boston and the neighboring towns. The Blue Hills were much more visited in those days than now, when the summit of Mount Washington is hardly a day's journey from Boston.

The other ancient houses in Milton belong to a later period and to a much higher style of architecture. The Foye house, now occupied by Mr. Samuel Littlefield, the Hutchinson house, better known to the present generation as the Russell house, the Inman or Robbins house on Brush Hill, the Taylor house, between the two churches, and the Gov. Belcher place (his house was burned in 1776,) are not only in themselves among the finest places in this neighborhood, but they have also associations of historical interest. Gov. Hutchinson's house, as Mr. Robbins informs me, was confiscated after he fled from the country. It was purchased by Samuel Broom, and, passing from his hands, became the residence of James Warren, whose wife, Mercy Warren, was the author of a valuable history of our revolutionary war. Thomas Lee of Cambridge owned it for a little while, and sold it to Patrick Jeffrey who had married Madam Haley, a sister of the noted John Wilkes of England. Jeffrey's wife left him, and he died at his house in Milton, in 1812. The estate was afterwards purchased by Mr. Barney Smith, and is now owned by his grandchildren, the heirs of his daughter, the late Mrs. Lydia S. Russell, widow of the Hon. Jonathan Russell.

Maj. General EDWIN VOSE SUMNER, [see p. 6,] son of Elisha and Nancy [Vose] Sumner, was born in Boston where his father resided a few years But both his parents were natives of Milton to which they returned while he was yet a child. They lived in the house now occupied by Miss Kendall on the right hand side of the Canton road, next beyond the lane that leads to the top of Brush Hill.

## OFFICERS NOW IN THE WAR.

The following officers from Milton are now actively engaged in the war. Those who know them best have the least apprehension that they will bring any thing but honor to the town or to the august and sacred cause to which they are giving themselves. And the same may be said of many of our young men who have gone as privates.

Lewis N. Tucker, Capt. Co. A. 18th Reg. Mass. Volunteers. John E. White, Capt. Co. G. 99th Reg. N. Y. Volunteers. Algernon S. Badger, 1st Lieutenant, Co. I. 26th Reg, Mass. Volunteers. Walter S. Davis, 1st Lieutenant, Co. F. 22d Reg. Mass. Volunteers. William H. Forbes, 1st Lieutenant, 1st Reg. Mass. Cavalry. Stephen G. Perkins, 1st, Lieutenant, Co. H. 2d Regiment, Mass Volunteers. Edward S. Huntington, 2d Lieutenant, 11th U. S. Infantry.

Since the above was written, one of these young men, Stephen G. Perkins, has fallen in battle at Cedar Mountain. He was one of the finest examples that I have known of manly integrity, and purity of heart. It would not be easy to find a man who had less taste for the excitement, the glory, or the pursuits of war. He went not from impulse, but from a deliberate sense of duty. His thought had always been more for others than for himself. He was reserved and undemonstrative in his manners. His actions were better than his words, but his character was greater and better than either. He grew upon his associates from day to day, till he became in himself an influence among them, so that they felt, as one of them expressed it, that they must all have higher purposes of life, because they had lived with him. His eye was as clear as the eye of an infant, and every morning found him apparently as new and fresh as if he had just been made.

> " Thy soul was like a star and dwelt apart :
>     \*    \*    \*    \*    and yet thy heart
> The lowliest duties on herself did lay."

It is a great price that we are paying for our civil rights, but the institutions which produce such men are worth defending at any cost, and the country which has such young men to give is worth dying for.

Lieutenant Perkins was the son of Stephen H. Perkins, and grandson of Samuel G. Perkins. His mother was the daughter of Richard Sullivan. He was graduated at Harvard College in 1856, and at first studied law. But some things in the practice of the law offended his sensitive moral nature, and he entered the Scientific School at Cambridge, where he had just completed the course and taken his degree, when he went off to join the 2d Mass. Regiment.

## PETER THACHER.

Peter Thacher, son of Rev. Thomas Thacher, first minister of the Old South Church in Boston, according to Dr. Sprague, Annals of American Pulpit 1. p.

196, was born in Salem, in the year 1651. His mother was a daughter of Rev. Ralph Partridge of Duxbury. He was graduated at Harvard College, in 1671, where he was the classmate and friend of the first Chief Justice Sewall. He was a tutor at Cambridge several years, and instructed the class of which Cotton Mather was a member. He became the intimate friend of his classmate and fellow tutor, Samuel Danforth, son of the Deputy Governor, whom he accompanied to England, soon after leaving college. While in England he was strongly urged to join the Established Church, and tempting offers were made to him. But after careful investigation, his mind was made up against the claims of the church of England, and soon after the death of his friend, Mr. Danforth, near the end of 1676, he returned home. See Savage's Genealogical Dictionary, vol. 1, p. 272. "He married," says Mr. Savage, "21st Nov., 1677, Theodora, daughter of Rev. John Oxenbridge of the First Church, which had eight years before been in fierce enmity with the third church founded for his father, and so, I hope, some help was given to the quiet that began, soon after the death of Gov. Bellingham, to reign through the colony so long disturbed." They had nine children, only three of whom survived their father. She died 18th Nov. 1697, and he, for his second wife, married Susannah, widow of Rev. John Bailey, assistant minister at the First Church, Boston. They had one child who died in infancy. She died 4th Sept., 1724, in her 59th year. In 1727, about three months before his death, he married Elizabeth, daughter of Judah Thacher, and widow of the first Joshua Gee, and not of Rev. Joshua Gee, who, Mr. Savage says, survived him by many years. Peter Thacher, according to the Church records, was ordained in Milton, 1st June, 1681, and died 17th Dec., 1727. The funeral sermon by Cotton Mather is a beautiful discourse, and the title is as follows :

"The comfortable chambers opened and visited, upon the departure of that aged and faithful servant of God, Mr. Peter Thacher, the never to be forgotten pastor of Milton, who made his flight thither, on December 17, 1727."

The Boston Weekly Journal of 23d Dec., 1727, thus speaks of him : "He was a person of eminent sanctity, of a most courteous and complaisant behavior; cheerful, affable, humble and free of speech to the meanest he met with. He had a great deal of vivacity in his natural genius, which, being tempered with grace and wisdom, appeared very engaging both in his common converse and public performances. In his ordinary conversation there was a vein of piety, agreeably mingled with entertaining turns and passages, an air of freedom and cheerfulness, that made it very easy and pleasant in any company. * * He was a zealous asserter of the purity and liberty of our evangelical churches."

Peter Thacher's daughter Theodora, who was admitted to the Church in Milton, Feb. 2, 1701, married Capt Jonathan Gulliver, and died Dec. 7, 1732. The following is from Mr. Thacher's Church Records : "March 23, 1700 or 1701. Son Oxenbridge, Daughter Elizabeth, Mercy and Mary Badcock were admitted into full communion with the church in Milton." His son, Peter Thacher joined the church, Feb. 6, 1704. Oxenbridge was born in Milton, May 17, 1681, and was graduated at Harvard College, 1698. In 1713-4 he married

Elizabeth Lillie, sister of Sir Charles Hobbie. She died Nov. 3, 1736, aged 61. He married (2) Bathsheba Kent, widow of John, July 30, 1740. In 1737 he was residing in Boston, as at that time he was dismissed from the church in Milton, and "recommended to Dr. Sewal's Church in Boston." I do not know how long he continued in Boston, but he spent the last years of his life in Milton, where he died, Oct. 29, 1772, at the great age of 91 years, 5 months, and 12 days. He must long have been the patriarch of the town.

His son Oxenbridge, grandson of Rev. Peter Thacher, was a man of extraordinary influence and ability. He was graduated at Harvard College in 1738, and for many years no man in Boston held a higher place at the bar. He entered with all his heart into the contest with England, and was associated with James Otis and John and Samuel Adams in the discussions with which that contest began. He died however in 1765, ten years before the war had actually broken out. John Adams gives the following vivid sketch of him. "From 1758 to 1765, I attended every superior and inferior court in Boston, and recollect not one in which he did not invite me home to spend evenings with him, when he made me converse with him as well as I could on all subjects of religion, mythology, cosmogony, metaphysics,——Locke, Clarke, Leibnitz, Bolingbroke, Berkley,—the preëstablished harmony of the universe, the nature of matter and of spirit, and the eternal establishment of coincidences between their operations, fate, foreknowledge, knowledge absolute,— and we reasoned on such unfathomable subjects, as high as Milton's gentry in pandemonium ; and we understood them as well as they did, and no better. But his favorite subject was politics, and the impending threatening system of parliamentary taxation, and universal government over the colonies. On this subject he was so anxious and agitated, that I have no doubt it occasioned his premature death."

The second Oxenbridge Thacher married Sarah Kent, probably the daughter of his step-mother, July 27, 1741, and had eight children. Of these, two entered the ministry and were greatly distinguished in their day; viz. Peter, born in Milton, where he was baptized, March 15, 1752, and Thomas. Peter was graduated at H. C., 1769. He was first settled in Malden, and in January, 1785, was settled over the Brattle Street Church in Boston, and was greatly distinguished for his personal virtues and his persuasive eloquence. His brother Thomas (H. C. 1775) was the minister of West Dedham, and was never married. He was an eccentric, able man, and used to say, "I know, brother Peter excels me in prayer, but I can give the best sermons." Peter was made a D. D. by the University of Edinburg, and died in Savannah, Ga., in the autumn of 1802. October 8, 1770, he married the widow Elizabeth Pool, and had ten children. His son, Thomas Cushing, was the minister of Lynn. Another son, Peter Oxenbridge, was a judge of the Boston Municipal Court. "In the difficult and often critical exercise of the powers entrusted to him," says President Quincy, "he upheld the dignity of his office, and maintained the cause of justice with a fearless and discriminating spirit." A younger son, Samuel Cooper, the successor of Rev. John T. Kirkland as pastor

of the New South Church, in Boston, May, 1811, the intimate friend of Buck-
minster and Channing, was a man greatly beloved and honored. He died at
Moulins, in France, January 2, 1818, and his body now rests, with that of his
father, in the burying-ground in Milton. A beautiful Memoir of his life was
written by his friend and successor in the ministry, Rev. F. W. P. Greenwood.

I remember another descendent of our Peter Thacher, who deserves to be
mentioned here as a most worthy minister. Rev. William Vincent Thacher
(H. C. 1834.) was a minister in Savannah, Ga., for a short time, and gained
the entire confidence of those who knew him. He died on his passage from
Savannah to Boston, in 1839. He, too, I think, is buried with many of his
family, in our Milton grave-yard.

## JOHN TAYLOR.

John Winslow, of Plymouth, born in 1597, the son of Edward Winslow, of
England, and brother of the distinguished Edward Winslow of Plymouth, came
to Plymouth in the Fortune, 1623, and in 1627 married Mary, daughter of
James Chilton. There is a family tradition that she was the first person of
English parentage who landed in the expedition to Plymouth ; she having
leaped from the boat and waded ashore. This tradition was written down in
1769, from the lips of her grand-daughter, Ann [Winslow] Taylor, then in her
92nd year. Their son Edward Winslow, by his second wife, Elizabeth, (d. of
the second Edward Hutchinson and his wife,Catharine Ham by, d. of a lawyer
at Ipswich, Eng.,) had, among other children, Ann, born Aug. 7, 1678, who
married John Taylor, and was the mother of Rev. John Taylor, the minister
of Milton. Of John, the father, who died in Jamaica, nothing is known except
that he was the son of Richard Taylor, of Boston, who joined the church Jan.
1, 1642, being then "a single man and a tailor." Richard, by his wife Mary,
had John, born the 2nd, baptized the 6th of February, 1647, and died in 1673.
Having sustained a good character in life, he was lamented in death. "He,"
says his daughter-in-law, "bequeathed two handsome legacies to the old
Brick and Old South Churches in Boston."

The Rev. John Taylor, of Milton, was born in 1703, and was graduated at
Harvard College in 1721, being the class-mate of Chief-Justice Stephen Sewall, as his predecessor, Peter Thacher, had been the class-mate of C. J. Sam'l
Sewall, fifty years before. He was ordained in Milton, Nov. 13, 1728, Rev.
Thomas Foxcraft, of Boston, preaching the sermon ; and died Jan. 26, 1750.
One of his daughters married Nicholas Gilman, of Exeter, N. H., and was the
mother of John Taylor Gilman, a man of sound judgment and massive integrity
of character, who was 13 years governor of N. H. Her son Nicholas Gilman
was a Senator in Congress, a man of great personal influence, and an accomplished gentleman. Her son Nathaniel Gilman was also a man widely known
and respected. This family of Gilmans has been one of the most distinguished
families in N. H.

Rev. John Taylor built the pleasant house, which now stands between the
two churches in Milton, and which is occupied by Capt. Charles Taylor,

and his sisters, whose mother, Mrs. Mary Taylor, who lived in this house till her death, March 16, 1860, aged 89, was the widow of William Taylor, the son of that William Taylor who was the nephew of the minister and wrote down his grandmother's words. She retained her faculties to the last, and was able to tell more about what had taken place here during the last eighty years than any other person that I knew. Her memory of things was very exact and vivid. She had a sound, discriminating mind, and was of a retiring, modest disposition. There was a quiet dignity about her which was very pleasing. She was one of the finest representatives among us of a generation which has now passed away.

As to the tradition respecting Mary Chilton, the words given below were written down by William Taylor, in September, 1769, "as related," he says, "by my grandmother, Madam Ann Winslow,' who was born the 7th of Aug. and baptized the 8th of Dec., 1678, which was the year before Mary [Chilton] Winslow died, and only 58 years after the landing at Plymouth. Ann Winslow's mother, Elizabeth Hutchinson, was born in 1639. She was forty years the contemporary of Mary Chilton, and for ten years, at least, her daughter-in-law; so that Ann Winslow had abundant means of learning whether the story was true or not. Mr. Savage says in regard to it, Genealogical Dic., IV., p. 604 : "She [Mary Chilton] had come in the Mayflower, and in her favor circulates the ridiculous tradition that she was the first of English parentage that leapt on Plymouth Rock ; but the worthless glory is equally well or ill claimed for John Alden, for neither of them is entitled to that merit." I agree with Mr. Savage as to the value of the glory. But it will be seen that the family tradition is not that she first " leapt on Plymouth Rock." Mr. Taylor's memoranda of what his grandmother said is as follows : " She [Mary Chilton] came over with her father and mother and other adventurers to this new settlement. One thing worthy of notice is that her curiosity of being first on the North American strand, prompted her, like a young heroine, to leap out of the boat and wade ashore. John Winslow, another early adventurer, married said Mary Chilton, from whom have descended a numerous and respectable posterity. My grandmother, now living, who affords me these memoirs, is the last surviving grandchild, in the 92nd year of her age."

## REV. NATHANIEL ROBBINS.

Stories are still told which show the easy and familiar terms on which Mr. Robbins lived with his people, and their friendly relations to him. From 1770 to 1785, or even later, was a period of great privation and distress among our people. At no time since the first years of the Plymouth Colony has the condition of the ministry been more circumscribed and embarrassing. For example, Rev. Samuel West, D. D., of the second precinct in Dartmouth, now New Bedford and Fair Haven, was one of the ablest and most faithful ministers of that generation. But in January, 1779, in consequence of representations from persons " of undoubted veracity, that the circumstances" of Mr. West " were in such a degree deplorable as to demand immediate relief," a meeting of the precinct was called, and it was voted to raise seventy pounds to procure fire-wood and corn for Mr. West. In most of the country parishes throughout New England there was the same distress, growing out of the depreciated and disordered state of the currency, and the disturbed condition of the country. Mr. Robbins was too skillful a farmer to be reduced to such straits as many of his brethren were, but the voluntary contributions of his parishioners, in those trying times, must have formed no unimportant part of his income from the parish. Mr. Robbins's son, Edward Hutchinson Robbins, Lieut. Governor of Massachusetts, and many years Judge of Probate for Norfolk County, during the latter years of the last century and the first quarter of this, exercised a more important influence in this town than any other man. His death is thus mentioned in our Church Records: "Dec. 29, 1829, Hon. E. H. Robbins. The eldest son of the late Rev. Nath'l Robbins. A great man has fallen in our Israel."

## REV. JOSEPH McKEAN.

In strength of mind, in earnestness of purpose, in intellectual accomplishments, in a high sense of honor and of duty, Mr. McKean was certainly inferior to no one of the honored men who preceded or followed him in the ministry here. But he came here very young. Our national government was not yet fairly embarked. The cries of party warfare were for the first time fiercely assailing it, and he threw himself into its defence with all the ardor of a generous and inexperienced youth. He was greatly beloved here. Between leaving H. C. in 1794 and settling here in 1797, he had taught an academy at South Berwick, Me. A venerable man, now living, has told me that he was one of his pupils there, and that, at the close of the last term, every pupil had a glass of wine put into his hand, and the teacher, with a glass in his hand, proposed this toast: "The rising generation: may they continue to rise till they all meet in heaven." After Mr. McKean had his connection with the parish dissolved, his family remained in Milton several years. He married Amy Swasey, of Ipswich, and left three sons: Joseph William, Henry Swasey, John George. They all graduated at H. C., and were young men of uncommon ability, but died too soon to fulfil entirely the promise of their early youth. Of the daughters, one married Joseph E. Worcester, LL. D., and another Charles Folsom, A. M. Both are now living in Cambridge.

## THE VOSE FAMILY.

"Aunt Sarah," the widow alluded to on p. 13, was Sarah [Bent] Vose, widow of Elijah Vose, and numbering among her descendants, until the present war, every one connected with Milton who has been most distinguished for military ability. Besides her four sons already mentioned as engaged in our Revolutionary war, her grandson, Josiah Howe Vose was a Colonel in the U. S. Army. His eldest son, Josiah H. Vose, received an appointment as Lieut. in the U. S. A. in 1838; but his constitution, naturally delicate, was unequal to the hardships and exposures to which he was subjected in the Florida war. A sick leave was obtained, and, in the 25th year of his age, he died in New York, June 20, 1841, just eighteen hours after his arrival there. Charlotte C., daughter of Col. Josiah H. Vose, married T. O. Barnwell, of the U. S. A., and died at Fort Towson, Choctaw Nation, Sept. 9, 1836, aged 23. Her sister, Elizabeth, married George P. Field, then Lieut., afterwards a Captain in the U. S. A. He was born at Black Rock, near Buffalo, Nov. 11, 1813. He entered the Military Academy, at West Point, in 1829, and on graduating was attached to the Infantry. He was engaged in the war with the Seminoles, and afterwards in the Mexican war. He distinguished himself in the battles of the Rio Grande, and fell at Monterey, at the head of his company, while gallantly engaged with the enemy. Captain Field was not only a brave officer, but a thoughtful, religious-minded, Christian man. His only son, Josiah Howe Vose Field, has just entered on the last year of his course in the West Point Military Academy. Col. J. H. Vose's sister Naomi married Joseph Heath, of Roxbury, son of the distinguished Gen. William Heath ; and his sister, Nancy, married Elisha Sumner, and became the mother of Edwin Vose Sumner, now Major General of Volunteers, and Brigadier General by Brevet in the U. S. A.

Col. Joseph Vose, "Aunt Sarah's" son, was born in 1738, and, Nov. 5, 1761, married Sarah Howe, daughter of Josiah Howe, a shoemaker, who moved from Dorchester to Milton when Sarah was two years old, and lived in the old house next to the burying ground. Joseph Vose was a butcher, engaging in the business when a very young man. He carried his meat to market every day, going early in the morning and returning late at night, so that sometimes he did not see his children from Sunday to Sunday. He built what is now the Vose house, on the old Vose place, but a few rods distant from the spot where "Aunt Sarah" lived, her house being much nearer the brook. Joseph was the Colonel, and Elijah the Lieut. Colonel, of the 1st Mass. Reg., and both distinguished themselves in Washington's army in New Jersey. Moses and Bill served in a more humble capacity, but with a zeal and fidelity which demand our gratitude and respect.

Col. Elijah had two children, Hon. Elijah Vose, of Boston, whose son, Hon. Henry Vose, is now a Judge in our Superior Court, and Ruth, the wife of Eben Breed, of Charlestown. Col. Joseph Vose, who died in 1816, aged 77, had eleven children. Sarah was married to Dr. George Osgood, of Andover, Mass. Margaret was married to Ezekiel Savage, then of Boston. Solomon died at Augusta, Maine, in 1809. Dolly and Nancy were twins ; the former married Davis Sumner, and the latter married his brother, Elisha Sumner. Naomi married Joseph Heath, of Roxbury, son of Gen'l Heath. Joseph died unmarried, in August 1825. Isaac was a merchant in New Orleans, and died in Boston. Elijah died when a child. Elizabeth Eliot is now living. Colonel Josiah H. Vose, the youngest son, was born in Milton, Aug. 8, 1784, and died in New Orleans, at the U. S. Barracks, July 15, 1845. He "was on parade, engaged in drilling his regiment, when he became suddenly indisposed, and after turning over his command to the next senior officer, retired to his quarters, which he had just reached when he fell dead upon the floor. He was 61 years of age, and had been more than 33 years in the service of his country ; having been commissioned as a Captain of Infantry in 1812, and passed with honor through every grade from that to his present rank." Both as an able officer and as an upright, kind-hearted man, he was esteemed and trusted while he lived, and died lamented and beloved.

The first of the Vose family in Milton, so far as I can learn, was Robert, who, in 1654, purchased the estate now owned by the heirs of Col. Josiah H. Vose. He died Oct. 16, 1683, aged 84. His son Edward died Jan. 29, 1716, aged 80. A portion of the land which he had from his father, near the south foot of Brush Hill, is now owned by his descendants, in the family of the late Jesse Vose, senior. Nathaniel, son of Edward, was born Nov. 17, 1672, and died October, 1753. At the age of 24 he married Mary Belcher, by whom he had six children : Mary, 1697, (she died young,) Nath'l, jr., 1699, Jerusha, 1702, admitted into Church Dec. 30, 1716, (she married Andrew McKay,) Merriam (admitted into Church January 10, 1725, and married Moses Billings), Elijah, 1707, (baptized Jan. 4. 1708,) Millatiah, baptized June 25, 1719, (she married Henry Crane.) The last name is Millatiah in the Milton Ch. records, but Mehitabel in the family records.

Elijah was the husband of "Aunt Sarah," and his father, Capt. Nathaniel, seems to have been considered the patriarch of the family by all his descendants. Nath'l and his wife, Mary, were admitted into Church, Dec. 4, 1698. He died Oct., 1753. According to a paper, kindly put into my hands by a member of the family, " He was a New England Puritan in faith and practice, using great self-denial, and educating his children in the most rigid manner of his sect. He ministered daily at the family altar, and continued to do so during the twilight of his life, which was passed in the family of his younger son. Early upon the Sabbath morning, would he summons his daughter to the holy duties of the day by loudly proclaiming at their doors that the holy women were early at the sepulchre. But upon other mornings, he left them to their rest. Among the last recollections of his favorite grandson, Col. Joseph Vose, was the 17th chapter of Jeremiah, which he used to repeat to his children as being the favorite morning lesson for the Sabbath ; he having learned it some seventy years before, while sitting on the cricket at his grandfather's feet, listening to the family exercise. From his frequent reading and quoting from the Scriptures, he was often called "the walking Bible." As a tiller of the soil, he was so successful that his name has been handed down to the present generation as ' Farmer Vose.' "

No one in our day would be so well entitled to this last name as Mr. Jesse Vose, of Brush Hill, who died Feb. 15, 1862. " I considered him," said a most competent judge, " the best farmer in Milton." But this was only one of his claims to respect. He united in himself many of the best qualities of his family. He was intelligent and faithful, modest and reserved. He was constant in his attendance on public worship, and yet a man of deeds more than of professions. As a son. a husband and a father, few have been more trusted and loved. As a neighbor, he was more ready to do a kind act than to talk about it ; and no one's advice was more sought and valued by those who needed it. The words most fitly describing him were : "What doth the Lord require of thee, but to do justly, and to love mercy, and to walk humbly with thy God ! "

## AGED PERSONS IN MILTON.

The person here alluded to on p. 22, was Mr. James Tucker, who died June 14, 1851. He was a Brush Hill farmer, an honest, clear-headed man, and one of the best representatives of his class. There was a shrewdness in his way of viewing things and a quaintness in his turn of expression, which gave an air of originality to his conversation, and made it always interesting. There was something very touching in his devotion to the memory of his wife, with whom he had lived so many years.

His cousin, Rev. Ebenezer Tucker, who died at the house of his son-in-law, Mr. Timothy Tucker, Jan. 14, 1848, aged 85, was graduated at Harvard College in 1783. He was a minister in Gerry, now Phillipston, till his failing health obliged him to give up his profession. After residing elsewhere more than sixty years, he came back to his native place, to spend his last days with his daughter and her family. He soon began to fail in body and mind till both seemed almost gone. But a little while before he died, believing that his hour had come, he called the family round him, and gave them his dying charge, talking to them nearly an hour and a half with great clearness and force on their Christian duties ; when he sunk back again into his previous oblivious state, only at intervals having consciousness enough to express his desire to go home and be at rest

Deacon Edward Capen, who died October 19, 1860, aged 85, lived near these men, and was connected with them by marriage He was a modest, kind-hearted, faithful man, and retained his strength of body and mind in a remarkable degree, down to his last illness. During the last year of his life, he not unfrequently walked to church, a distance of two miles, and back again when the services were ended.

Nearly opposite to Deacon Capen, Simon Ferry and his wife, Rhoda, lived together nearly fifty-four years — sensible, affectionate, thoughtful people. " My mind," he once said to me, with his characteristic modesty, " is simple in knowledge " But he had evidently thought much, especially on religious subjects, and his singleness of purpose had certainly led him further into the truth than some men of superior intellects ever go He died Nov. 10, 1857, aged 78, and she, Nov. 18, 1860, aged 73. She was married before she was seventeen.

Among the aged, though not the most aged men of Milton, when I came here in Jan. 1846, was the Hon. John Ruggles. He was an upright, intelligent man, decided in his opinions, and spoke like one who was accustomed, as he had been, to have his opinions respected. He was born in Milton, Feb. 10, 1773, in the house now occupied by Mr. John Myers, and died Dec. 19, 1846. His wife, who died Sept. 6 1857, was Betsy Wadsworth, and was born in Danvers, July 4, 1777. She used to say, playfully, that her birth-day had always been celebrated throughout the land. They were married in Danvers, Nov. 5, 1805, by her father, Rev. Benjamin Wadsworth, and were the parents of three children, the oldest of whom, Mary Wadsworth, died in infancy. There have been in Mr. Ruggles's family five successive generations of only sons, all bearing the name of John Ruggles, and the youngest, who now bears it, is the eighth John Ruggles in lineal succession. Both Mr. and Mrs. Ruggles were direct descendants of Deacon John Wadsworth, younger brother of Rev. Benjamin Wadsworth, who was graduated at Harvard College in 1690, and President of the College from 1725 to 1737. Mrs. Ruggles's father, Rev. Benj. Wadsworth, was born in Milton, July 18, 1750, graduated at H. C. in 1769, ordained Minister of the first parish in Danvers Dec. 23, 1772, made D. D. at H. C., 1816, and died January 18, 1826, having been the minister of his parish more than fifty-three years. He was a man greatly respected by his brethren in the ministry.

Mr Ruggles's father was chosen Town Treasurer of Milton in 1785, which office he held by annual election till his death, Feb. 25, 1821,—thirty-six years, lacking a few days. He was chosen Town Clerk in 1786, and continued in that office till March, 1807,—21 years. Mr. Ruggles himself was chosen Selectman in March, 1805, and remained in the office till March, 1826—twenty-one years ; and from 1811, fifteen years he was chairman of the board. He was also chairman of the board of Selectmen from 1830 to 1835,—making the whole number of years he held the office twenty-six, twenty of which he was chairman. He was one of the Assessors twenty-five years, and chairman nineteen. He was first chosen Town Clerk in 1814, and held that office till 1835, twenty-one years, when he declined further service in town offices. "It is a notable circumstance," says Mr. Jason Reed, our present Town Clerk, "that for precisely fifty years continuously, Mr. Ruggles and his father held important town offices ; for forty-two of these years they together held the office of Town Clerk, and for twenty-three years important town offices at the same time." Mr. Ruggles was representative to the Massachusetts General Court seven years, and State Senator five years, from 1820 to 1824.

Mr. and Mrs. Ruggles lived together more than forty-one years. I think the last word he was heard to utter was "Eternity," as if he were already looking into its mysterious and awful depths. His wife, who survived him nearly eleven years, was of a sensitive, delicate nature, and very humble in her religious feelings. She was a woman of strong personal attachments, and faithfully and wisely fulfilled the duties of a Christian wife and mother.

## RUGGLES.

1. Thomas came from England and settled in Roxbury with his son,
2. John, then about 12 years of age.
3. John,                                        of Roxbury.
4. John,                                        "       "
5. Capt John and Katherine (Williams).   "       "

6. Capt. John and Mary (Wadsworth) ; he removed to Milton.

7. Hon. John and Betsy (Wadsworth).

8. Betsy (Ruggles) Davenport and John ; the former married Francis W. Davenport, of Milton, the Davenports being early settlers of that town ; the latter married Mary L. Gardner, daughter of Hon. S. P. Gardner, of Bolton.

9. Mary Gardner and John.

## WADSWORTH.

1. Christopher, one of the early Plymouth Pilgrims, settled at Duxbury, with Miles Standish ; had by wife Grace, Joseph, John, Samuel and Mary.

2. Capt Samuel, born at Duxbury about 1630, married Abigail, daughter of James Lindall, of Marshfield ; appears at Milton, 1656 ; killed at Sudbury, 1676.

3. Dea. John, born 1674, died 1733–4, and Eliz. (Vose) ; they had eleven children.

4. Deacon Benjamin, born 1707, died 1771, and Esther (Tucker); they had ten children. Their house was standing a few years since at "Scotch Woods."

5 Rev. Benj. and Mary (Hobson). Also, Mary, married to Captain John Ruggles.

6. Betsy, married to Hon John Ruggles.

The six oldest inhabitants of Milton whose funerals I have attended, were :

Miss Sally Tucker who died Nov. 29, 1849, aged 93,

Mrs. Rebecca Howe who died Oct. 4, 1858, aged 86,

Miss Mary Crane who died Jan. 10, 1860, aged 95,

Miss Mary Vose who died Feb. 18, 1860, aged 86,

Mrs. Mary Taylor who died March 16, 1860, aged 89,

Mrs Sally Penniman who died Nov. 14, 1860, aged 86.

All of these, it will be noticed, were women ; and half the number, including the two oldest, had never been married. With the exception of Miss Crane, whose mind had been clouded for some years before her death, and, perhaps, Miss Vose, they all retained their faculties to the last, and kept up their interest, not only in the generations that had passed away, but in the living world around them. Four of the six died in the same year.

## THE FAMILY OF RUFUS PIERCE.

The allusion p. 23 is to the family of Rufus Pierce, son of William and Eunice (Bent) Pierce. He was born in 1751, and married Elizabeth Howe, daughter of Josiah Howe and sister of Sarah (Howe), wife of Colonel Joseph Vose. Josiah Howe was engaged in the shoe-making business, on what was then considered a large scale. He died October 3, 1792, aged 73 When our Revolutionary war with England broke out, he became very much depressed, and, like some faint-hearted or despondent persons now, he could see no prosperous issue out of the sad and troubled times in which he lived. His son, Josiah Howe, removed to Templeton, and was the father of Josiah Howe, M. D., a physician of considerable distinction and ability in Westminster. The children of Rufus and Elizabeth Pierce were, Elizabeth, born Oct. 19, 1775, married, Nov. 30, 1817, William Briggs, and still living in the house built and occupied by her father,—Lemuel, born Feb. 9, 1778,—Sarah, born July 16, 1780, married, March 10, 1803, Samuel Littlefield,—Margaret, born April 29, 1783, married Jeremiah T. Fenno, died August 14, 1857,—Eunice, now Mrs. Lord, born Feb. 24, 1787.—Nancy, born July 13, 1790, married Gideon F. Thayer, the eminent teacher, died Nov. 21, 1854,—Mary, born Dec. 5, 1795, married Zipheon Thayer, died May 14, 1837,—Rufus, born March 31, 1798, now living in Illinois,—and Martha, born July 16, 1801, married Abel Wyman, and died April 1836. Mary was the person of whom Dr. Channing spoke.

## ANN BENT.

Miss Ann Bent's grandfather was Alexander Middleton, a Scotchman who lived in Boston. He left four daughters : Mary Middleton, who married James Lovell, son of " Master Lovell." She was Mrs Henry Ware's grandmother. She had several sons, only one daughter, Mary, who married Mr. Mark Pickard. Gen. Mansfield Lovell, of New Orleans, is her great grand-son. Ann Middleton married Rufus Bent, who was born in Milton, one of four brothers—Joseph, Lemuel, William and Rufus. Their only sister was Eunice, who married William Pierce, and was the grandmother of Mrs. Elizabeth Briggs. Rufus and Ann Bent lived in Milton and Boston. They had seven children,—two sons, who died at sea, and five daughters. He died at his daughter's in Canton, in 1807, and his wife, at a daughter's in Dorchester Upper Mills in 1805. Prudence Middleton married Dr. Joseph Whipple, who lived in Boston. Ann Bent, the eldest of the five sisters, was born in Milton and died in Canton, (where she is buried,) in 1856, aged eighty-eight years and three months. Her parents were poor, and she went, when quite young, to live with Madam Price, an English lady who lived in Hopkinton. Mrs. Price was very kind to her, and she retained her friendship through life. She was there several years. She returned to Milton, took a school, lived in Judge Robbins's family, who lived in what is now the Churchill house, on Milton Hill for three years. His three eldest children attended her school. She was very much attached to the whole family, and retained their esteem and friendship during her life. In 1795 she found a more lucrative position in Boston. She took the store, 56 Marlboro' Street,where W. H. Allen's store in Washington Street now is. Messrs. Gregory and Pickard (Mr. P. was Mrs. Ware's father,) stocked it with rich goods which they imported for her to sell on commission. Two of her sisters went into the store with her. They boarded with Mrs. Thayer (mother of Rev. Dr. Thayer, of Lancaster), in what is now Washington St., opposite Central Ct. Sally, the youngest sister, soon married Mr. Charles Barnard, who als boarded there. Miss Bent then purchased the building adjoining her store, and kept house, with her sister Mary to assist her. Nancy Pierce (afterward Mrs. G. F. Thayer), and Fanny Cushing (afterwards Mrs. Dr. Stone, of Greenfield, and mother of Gen. C. P. Stone, now at Fort Lafayette,) were her assistants. Her two oldest nieces, Ann Middleton Allen (now Mrs. Tracy) and Mary Bent Kinsley, girls of ten years, living with her, she sent to school. This formed her family for many years, with a domestic, Nabby Tower, who lived with her thirty years. The two assistants married, and the two nieces took their place. When they were seventeen years old, she put them in a position to assist their large families. She then took two more nieces into her family,—Ann Kingsley and Sarah Barnard Kingsley. Her sister Prudence married Mr. Silas Kingsley, of Canton, where she is now living, eighty-eight years old, and the last of her family.

A niece of Miss Bent, to whom I am indebted for most of these details, says of her, " The beauty and purity of my aunt's character no one knows better than myself. I lived in the most intimate relations with her for more than forty years. I never saw her do or heard her say anything that might not have been said or done before the whole world. In her business relations she was *perfection*, she was so high-minded and so just to everybody in her dealings and her estimation of character. She was a mother to her sisters and their children, ever thinking of their good." These were the qualities which made steadfast friends of those whose friendship was most to be sought, and formed for her a home in which she was never allowed to feel the loneliness of celibacy or age. The affluent, the educated and the refined valued her society, and were among her cherished friends. But there was a nearer circle yet. Children were drawn towards her, and as one generation of those to whom she had been as a mother left her to establish homes of their own, others, still younger took their place, and looked up to her with love and reverence. Thus her benefactions, performed with no selfish intent, returned into her own bosom. And those who were as dear to her as children and children's children delighted to do what they could to lighten for her the burden of increasing years, and to fill the atmosphere around her with the affections in which it was a joy for her to live. The example is one that cannot be too warmly commended.

## REPRESENTATIVE WOMEN OF MILTON.

Louisa Goddard Wigglesworth, the person described p. 28, was the daughter of Isaac and Mary [May] Davenport. Mr. Davenport was one of a family which had been in Milton, or at least in Dorchester, [See History of Dorchester,] almost from its earliest settlement He was born in Milton, and was for many years a merchant in Boston, the partner of John McLean. He left but two children, both daughters. Louisa was much younger than her sister and usually spent her winters in Boston. But her earliest associations bound her to Milton, where every knoll and stream and tree was dear to her. She loved the place for its own sake and for her father's sake. She was a liberal benefactor to the Church. She knew something about all the old Milton families, and kept up her interest in them as long as she lived.

She was married to Samuel Wigglesworth, M. D. in Boston, Dec. 7, 1841, Their eldest child, Samuel Norton, was born Aug. 23, 1845. Dr. Wigglesworth had already begun to suffer from a most painful disease. Her eye-sight had begun to fail, and she probably never saw their second son, Francis Thos., who was born on the 17th of September, 1846. Dr. Wigglesworth died the following spring, April 7, 1847. Her mother, the sister of Col. Joseph and Dea. Samuel May, of Boston, died Nov. 20, 1853, aged 84 years and 10 mos. Her son, Francis Thomas, a boy of unusual beauty and loveliness of character, died the 17th of April, 1854. Her cousin, Miss Catherine Davenport, who had always made a part of her father's family, died soon after. Still she did her part faithfully and well, performing duties from which others situated as she was, even without her loss of sight might have excused themselves and been unblamed. She took an interest in whatever occurred, and even in objects of natural scenery, which were described to her as she was passing them. She visited the White Mountains, and seemed really and heartily to catch the inspiration of the place, and to appreciate and enjoy the views around her. But as, from year to year, one object after another of interest and affection to her became detached from life, it was easy to see that her hold on life, both bodily and mental, was growing less. In March, 1859, she came out to Milton to attend the funeral of Josiah Cotton, a black man whom she had known from her earliest childhood as a servant in her father's household, and the last surviving member of that household. Her health soon after began to fail, and she died in Milton, July 17, 1859. Her only remaining son, Samuel Norton Wigglesworth, died the 15th of November, 1861.

There are other persons whom I should be glad to mention here,—women taken away in the prime of life, whose lives were a benefaction to the community, and whose names call up now tender and affecting memories. There was no duty too difficult to be performed by them with cheerfulness, or too humble to be made attractive by the grace which they bestowed upon it. Through their gracious and kindly interposition, in many cases, sickness lost much of its severity. Friendless women were sought out and made to feel that they were not alone in the world, or wholly shut out from its sympathy and advantages. They were steadfast and loyal in their friendships. One could hardly meet them without carrying away something which it was both refreshing and useful to remember. They loved to do a kind act for its own sake and not because of large returns that they were seeking from any philanthropical investment which they might make. No one who knew them would hesitate to apply to them for counsel or effective aid in any enterprize of mercy or beneficence that come, even by the most liberal interpretation of good neighborhood, within their sphere. They have passed away, but the scenes on which they looked are more beautiful, the places they loved are more sacred, and the work they did is more easy now because of the spirit in which they lived.

And there were others of an earlier generation, who lived out their four score years and more,—women of dignified personal bearing and of remarkable conversational powers. Blue Hill and Brush Hill and Milton Hill had their representative women,—ladies of the old school, who had not feared to improve their minds by substantial reading and thinking. In their personal deportment there was that combination of dignity and kindness which secures our respect at the same time that it gains our confidence and affection. A lasting impression was often made upon the young by their conversation, which was none the less attractive because it was instructive, nor any the less entertaining because it was always high-toned in sentiment, and touching often on great and important subjects. They recognized their obligations to the community in which they lived and to all its members. They were ready to do their part in sustaining all good institutions, and deserve especially to be remembered and imitated in their relations to the poor. The influx of destitute foreigners, a few years ago, rendered public measures necessary to meet the heavy and multiplied calls of charity. But already that emergency has subsided, and there is danger lest public societies and relief provided by law should so interpose themselves between us and the poor whom we have always with us as to do away the pleasant and mutually beneficent relations which formerly connected a thoughtful, charitable woman with the needy and suffering around her. The relation was not one entirely of dependence on their part and of charity on hers. Her superior intelligence assisted and guided them. She taught them to help themselves, and encouraged their self-respect by enabling them to feel that they were doing something for her in return for her kindness to them. There were thus cherished between the parties habits of personal intercourse, sustained by feelings of deference and kindness and gratitude, which gave her a salutary influence over them, and ministered to the happiness of all.

Women of this character, representatives of the high breeding and better thought of a former generation, were here when I came to Milton. They seemed less like fleeting individuals than settled institutions, or permanent features in the landscape. I could hardly approach one of them without a subdued sentiment of tenderness and reverence. It seemed to me sometimes as if I could see the history of a whole life-time written out on the countenance, in characters which pointed far back into the past, and forward to a sky all aglow with hopes of future reunion and recognition. The shadows of many years had fallen upon them ; but there were new lights kindled for them in heaven. If they connected us with the past, they drew us also towards the future. The birds that come together to prepare for their departure when the summer days are beginning to put on an autumnal hue, take our thoughts back to the pleasant season which has been gladdened by their songs, and lead them forward to the sunny lands where their joyful home shall be when our bleak coast is scourged by the winter storms. So do they—our aged and beloved ones—stand before us, as messengers about to depart for other lands, and we can hardly see them without having our thoughts carried on from the cares and fears which attend us here, to the serenity, and joy, and everlasting peace which await them there.

## MILTON NAMES.

A sketch of the different families of Milton, their changing features, position, influence and character, would be full of interest and instruction. To trace the history of those who have removed from this place and see how the same traits which have been recognized here are developed elsewhere, what new features grow out of them or are engrafted upon them by altered circumstances and relations, would be a profitable work, and if intelligently and thoroughly carried out, it might do something in a small way, to throw light on one of the most important questions of the age, the distinction of families and races, and the manner in which they are moulded by external influences so as to lose their separate characteristics and become absorbed into one another. Researches of this kind, to be of any value, must be exceedingly minute and comprehensive. But there is also a superficial, disconnected way of viewing the subject, which is not without its interest to those who are attached to the place and the people living in it.

Of the twelve persons who signed the original Church Covenant in Milton, four bore names, Newton, Holman and Blacke (William and Edward), which are no longer found here. Sumner, Clap, Lion and Swift still remain. The Sumners have been a numerous and influential family. And sixty years ago, I have been told, that at a Town Meeting in Milton, no public measure could be carried which was opposed by John Swift, the energetic head of an important family which is now represented here by only one male member. The remaining four signers of the Covenant all bore the name of Tucker. During Mr. Thacher's ministry, there was usually a Dea. Tucker, Senior, and a Dea. Tucker, Junior. At the present time, the Tuckers hold, probably, about the same rank in numbers and position. There are to-day two deacons of that name in Milton. The first of the name that I find here was Robert. Mr. Savage gives this account of him : " Robert, Weymouth, 1638, had Sarah, born 17 March, 1629, and, I think, Ephraim, Benjamin and Manasseh, besides possibly others, before or after removal. He was fined in 1640, for upbraiding James Britain, as a witness ; called him a liar and said he could prove it ; of which the character of Britain may lead us to think he might be right ; removed to Dorchester, that part which became in 1662 Milton, for which he was representative 1669-80 and 1." This Robert Tucker was the " Recorder for Milton," when the town was first incorporated. It is said, probably somewhat hyperbolically, that there have been times when the Tuckers and Voses combined could out vote all the rest of the town.

Of the 114 names which I find in Mr. Thacher's records of baptisms and admissions to the Church, 34 are still found here, and 78 are no longer represented by any man in Milton. I give below these 114 names in Mr. Thacher's somewhat peculiar orthography, marking with an asterisk those which are now extinct among us.

| | | | |
|---|---|---|---|
| Adams | Durant* | Hunt | Stimson* |
| Andrews* | Eastee* | Hunter* | Sumner |
| Atherton* | Eeles* | Jemmeson* | Swan |
| Badcock | Endicot* | Jordon* | Swetland* |
| Badlambs* | Everenden* | Jones | Swift |
| Bailey* | Field | Kelton* | Swinnerton* |
| Beal | Fenno | Kinsley* | Talbut* |
| Belcher* | Ford* | Langley* | Thacher* |
| Bent | Foster | Liscome* | Toleman |
| Bentlet* | Frissel* | MacKee* | Tompson* |
| Billings* | Ganzey or Garsey* | Man* | Triscot* |
| Black* | Glover* | Miller* | Trot* |
| Blake | Gold or Gould | Montgomery* | Tucker |
| Blair* | Gouliver* | Mooree* | Vose |
| Chandler | Graécian* | Mos (Morse ?) | Wadland* |
| Clap | Gregory* | Newton* | Wadsworth |
| Collin | Grosse* | Peirce | Wales |
| Craine* | Harper* | Pitcher* | Warren |
| Crehore | Haughton | Puffer* | Web |
| Dammon, or | Hayden* or | Rawson* | Weeks* |
| Damon* | Heiden | Redman* | Wheeler |
| Daniel* | Henshire* | Rider* | White |
| Davenport | Hersey* | Robards or Robers | Wier* |
| Davis | Hichborne* | Roy* | Williston* |
| Dean* | Holman* | Sawyer* | Witherbee* |
| Denmark* | Horton* | Scot | Witherton* |
| Dennis* | How* | Sheperd | Withinton* |
| Dickerman | Hubbard* | Smith | Woody* |
| Dike* | Hudson* | Spencer* | |

Of the 34 names still found in Milton, quite a number, e. g. Smith, Web and Warren, have died out in the old stock, and are now represented by those who are inhabitants here of a comparatively recent date. Not 30 of the 114 names recorded before 1727 are now perpetuated here by lineal descendants of those then living in the town. These simple facts show the migratory character of our most stable N. E. population. A few families, e. g. Babcock, Tucker, Vose, hold now, perhaps, nearly the place which they held at the beginning of the last century. Others, e. g. Gulliver, Crehore, Billings, Henshaw, Belcher, Ford, have either entirely disappeared, or are reduced to a single male member. And not only families, but races have disappeared. The names of Indians and Negroes appear on our Church records, but at this time I think there is not one Indian man or woman, nor one Negro family, in Milton.

Besides the names which I have given, and which belong to the first 65 years of our history as a town, there are families which have come into the town, exercised an important influence for a generation or two, and then disappeared.

Mr. Robbins has mentioned several such families. Gov. Belcher and Gov. Hutchinson, though, living in a measure apart from the surrounding inhabitants, were parishioners in this place, and attendants at this church. The Thachers were represented here in four generations. The names, Smith, Boies, Holbrook, Amory, Baldwin, recall to our older citizens the remembrance of families, which, though never numerous and now represented here by no living descendant, held once a high place among the families of Milton. The M'Leans, father and son, ought not to be omitted in any notice, however slight, of the prominent Milton families. John M'Lean was born at Georges, near Thomaston, Me., in 1761. His father, Hugh M'Lean, removed soon after to Milton, where he engaged, and at length became largely interested, in the business of paper-making. He lived in the house now occupied by Mr. George Hollingsworth, and died Dec. 1799, aged 75. John M'Lean, during the latter part of his life, was in partnership with Mr. Isaac Davenport. He died Oct. 16, 1823, aged 62. Both father and son are buried in Milton. John M'Lean will be honorably known, for many generations to come, as the munificent benefactor, if not the founder, of the M'Lean Asylum for the Insane, at Somerville, and of the Mass. General Hospital in Boston. He was also the founder of the M'Lean Professorship of Ancient and Modern History in Harvard University. He bequeathed to the Congregational Society in Milton, and also to that in Federal Street, Boston, two thousand dollars each, the income to be distributed annually to such persons, "not paupers," as the minister and deacons of the respective societies "should deem suitable for such relief." Few men have done more than he did permanently to relieve human suffering in some of its most aggravated forms, and no one better deserves to be held in grateful remembrance for the perpetual benefactions which his wisdom and benevolence have devised and carried out. Yet the way in which our citizens are most frequently reminded of him seems to savor a little of ostentation. The mile-stones on the Brush Hill turnpike bear this inscription, "J M'Lean, 1823." The common impression, I believe, is, that these mile-stones, with this inscription, were erected by himself. But it was not so. They were erected by Mr. Isaac Davenport, at Mr. M'Lean's request and expense, and as they were not finished till after Mr. M'Lean's death, Mr. Davenport had this inscription put upon them, as a sort of monumental testimonial to his friend and partner.

Here I close these brief, imperfect, shadowy memorials of a past, whose spirit goes with us where we go, and, under the guiding hand of God, has made us what we are. It is a false philosophy that would separate the living from the dead, and send the children of each generation, fatherless and motherless, into the world, to seek their fortunes, and to form their own characters. As we inherit our flesh and blood from our ancestors, so we are born into the ideas, sentiments, institutions, and habits which are the result of their living through many generations, and which we cannot change at pleasure by any arbitrary act of ours, but only as we change the quality of trees and plants, within certain limits, and in obedience to established laws. We grow out of the past. Its life flows through our veins. And yet we can modify that life. We can graft upon it better ideas. We can live amid what was low, parsimonious, and ungenerous in our ancestors, and perpetuate it with an added intensity and deformity of our own, or we can live amid what was lofty, disinterested, and praiseworthy in them, and thus help to purify and advance the tone of private and public sentiment in the community. It is with this purpose that I have taken a satisfaction, not wholly sad, though not entirely free from sadness, in walking, as it were, a little while among the graves, and calling up anew the forms of dear and honored ones, that, while moved and impressed by the memory of their virtues, I might soothe the feeling of personal bereavement by writing down their names, or, where that seemed too much an intrusion into the sacred privacy in which they moved, that I might at least refresh my own thoughts by the more inspiring images of holiness and piety which they furnish, and bind myself more firmly to heaven by the renewed affections which follow them into that higher realm.

To those who may look, a hundred years hence, at the church records which I have kept, there will appear only a catalogue of names. But to me almost every record that I have made recalls a scene which has its peculiar interest. Each wedding has its own little story of life's dearest hopes, fulfilled or disappointed. Each baptism calls up its own affecting image of the relation which the greatest artists have endeavored to express in their pictures, of the Madonna and her child, a new creation of God, to her at once the gift and the impersonation of the divine love. Each death, with the accompanying date and name, tells of a whole completed history, which, if it could be related in truthful, loving words, would be not without its interest and its uses even to strangers. I had wished to clothe some of these names with life again, that affections so gentle, hearts so true, countenances so beaming with intelligence and benignity, minds so thoughtful and so modest, a faith so humble and so lofty, a charity so gracious and self-forgetting, might not wholly perish in this place of their earthly abode, when those who knew and loved them here have all departed. But such things cannot be. We have our sainted dead, and those who come after us will have theirs. May we and they alike be true to the holiest memories which come to us from the past, till those memories become blended in our lives with the hopes which draw us on into a future still more beautiful and holy.

If a single copy of this pamphlet should, like a stray leaf on some troubled stream, be borne down to those who shall take part in the tri-centenary celebration of our town, we, from these sad times of civil war and present disasters, thus far bravely met and hopefully endured, would send them our kindly greeting, and our earnest prayer that they, under more peaceful skies and with greater fidelity and success, may labor, as we have sought to do, that the tabernacle of God may be with men, that he may dwell with them, and that they may be his people.

*Milton, Wednesday evening, Sept.* 10, 1862.

www.ingramcontent.com/pod-product-compliance
Lightning Source LLC
Chambersburg PA
CBHW031805090426
42739CB00008B/1173